LONDON MIDLAND
MAIN LINE CAMERAMAN

'Steam Past' Books from Allen & Unwin

THE LIMITED by O. S. Nock
THE BIRTH OF BRITISH RAIL by Michael R. Bonavia
STEAM'S INDIAN SUMMER by George Heiron and Eric Treacy
GRAVEYARD OF STEAM by Brian Handley
PRESERVED STEAM IN BRITAIN by Patrick B. Whitehouse
MEN OF THE GREAT WESTERN by Peter Grafton
TRAVELLING BY TRAIN IN THE EDWARDIAN AGE by Philip Unwin
MAUNSELL'S NELSONS by D. W. Winkworth
MAN OF THE SOUTHERN. JIM EVANS LOOKS BACK by Jim Evans
TRAINS TO NOWHERE: BRITISH STEAM TRAIN ACCIDENTS 1906–1960 by J. A. B. Hamilton
TRAVELLING BY TRAIN IN THE 'TWENTIES AND 'THIRTIES by Philip Unwin
MEN OF THE LNER by Peter Grafton
A HISTORY OF THE LMS by O. S. Nock:
    I. The First Years, 1920–30
    II. The Record-Breaking 'Thirties, 1931–39
    III. The War Years and the Finale, 1939–47
A HISTORY OF THE LNER by Michael R. Bonavia:
    I. The Early Years, 1923–33
    II. The Years of Achievement, 1934–39
    III. The Last Years, 1939–48
ON AND OFF THE RAILS by Sir John Elliot
THE RIDDLES STANDARD TYPES IN TRAFFIC by G. Freeman Allen
LONDON MIDLAND MAIN LINE CAMERAMAN by W. Philip Conolly
THE SCHOOLS 4–4–0s by D. W. Winkworth
SOUTH WEST RAILWAYMAN by Donald King
GREAT WESTERN LOCOMOTIVE DESIGN by John Gibson

STEAM, a year book edited by Roger Crombleholme and Terry Kirtland

LONDON MIDLAND MAIN LINE CAMERAMAN

W. Philip Conolly

Edited by Michael Esau

London
GEORGE ALLEN & UNWIN
Boston   Sydney

First published in 1982
Reprinted 1983

George Allen & Unwin (Publishers) Ltd,
40 Museum Street, London WC1A 1LU, UK

George Allen & Unwin (Publishers) Ltd,
Park Lane, Hemel Hempstead, Herts HP2 4TE, UK

Allen & Unwin Inc.,
9 Winchester Terrace, Winchester, Mass 01890, USA

George Allen & Unwin Australia Pty Ltd,
8 Napier Street, North Sydney, NSW 2060, Australia

British Library Cataloguing in Publication Data

Conolly, W. Philip
   London Midland main line cameraman.
   1. British Rail. *London Midland Region*—
   Pictorial works
   I. Title   II. Esau, Mike
   385′.0942   HE3020.B/

   ISBN 0-04-385099-5

Set in Goudy Old Style by Bedford Typesetters Ltd
and printed in Great Britain by
Biddles Ltd, Guildford, Surrey

INTRODUCTION

As a spectacle the steam locomotive at work had no rival in the realm of transport, a sight which has appealed to generations of railway lovers. Although locomotives were of principal interest, there was much else worthwhile to photograph, such as permanent way gangs at work, or signalling and signalmen, a little of which I have endeavoured to record over the years.

I started railway photography in 1926 with a folding camera, the name of which I have long forgotten, but I do recall that it had a 'Vario' shutter. During these first years I visited all the London termini, but found Euston to have the most attraction with its shining black and red locomotives, although even in pre-war days cleaning was not always carried out as often as it should have been, as some of my photographs show. Euston and St Pancras were the starting points for main line trains bound for places which excited my imagination and which one day I hoped to visit with my camera – Oxenholme, Tebay, Shap, Carlisle, or Ribblehead, Garsdale, Ais Gill and Kirkby Stephen on the Midland route.

In later years when the Public Relations Officer at Euston provided me with a lineside pass, I was able to enjoy the wonderful freedom of walking the cess for mile upon mile with my camera, by then a Corfield single lens reflex.

Around this time in the late 1940s and early 1950s, one had a wide variety of trains to photograph at locations such as Tebay, or Ais Gill to the east. Not only were there LNWR and Midland built locomotives at work, but also newly de-streamlined Duchess Pacifics, increasing numbers of rebuilt Scots and Patriots and, of course, the first Standard types.

The weather in the northern fells has ever been unpredictable, so quite often my pictures were taken in the driving rain which swept unhindered from the west – on one occasion I remember tipping the water out of my camera, but miraculously the film was unharmed! Without a nearby car for protection between trains, there was little shelter, but hot tea in a signal-box or ganger's hut cheered a dismal day no end. I made some good friends among the London Midland railwaymen, and some of them appear in this book.

Today, especially on the old LNWR main line to Carlisle, almost all the reminders of the steam age have gone, and even the Settle and Carlisle Midland route is under threat of closure. The popular 'Cumbrian Mountain Express' has kept the tradition of main line steam alive, but I hope my photographs will be a reminder of what the working steam railway was really like, and bring pleasure and interest to those who browse through these pages.

In conclusion I wish to thank Mike Esau for the splendid enlargements he has made from his selection of my negatives, and for putting the book together. Without his kind assistance and guidance it is doubtful if it would ever have been produced, for I disposed of my dark-room equipment at the end of steam.

W. PHILIP CONOLLY
Ewell, March 1982

With that wonderful 3-cylinder roar of a hard worked Jubilee, no. 45706, 'Express', climbs Shap near Scout Green. Confident in his free steaming engine, the driver contemplates the fells.

5

THE JOURNEY BEGINS

(*Above*) Adding to the grime of Carlisle station, Preston Jubilee no. 45599, 'Bechuanaland', pulls out with a Glasgow–Manchester train in 1948.

(*Above right*) Something of the atmosphere of Carlisle in steam days can be sensed in this picture of two class 5 4–6–0s waiting to leave for the south on a wet morning in June 1950.

(*Below right*) Luck played a part in my capturing this simultaneous departure of two Royal Scots from Euston in 1930. The one on the left is in charge of a parcels train, the other an express to Manchester.

EUSTON

(*Right*) In the late 1930s a Hughes 2–6–0 no. 2787 is ready to leave Euston for Willesden sidings with the empty stock of an overnight train from Scotland.

(*Below*) Dear old Euston as many people remember it; cramped, noisy, dirty, but full of character. The usual LNWR 0–8–0 waits to give its train a hefty push out of the platform one Sunday in 1946.

(Above) In the steam era spotters had a wide choice of London termini to visit, though Euston never seemed to be quite as popular as King's Cross. Jubilee class no. 45738, 'Samson' coasts in with a morning express from Birmingham.

(Below) The 'Shamrock' from Liverpool Lime Street at Euston at the end of its journey behind Princess Royal Pacific no. 46211, 'Queen Maud'.

'SPOTTERS'

(*Right*) Some of the Saturday gallery of spotters and enthusiasts at Crewe enjoy a grandstand view from the footbridge at the north end of the station as Coronation Pacific no. 6254, 'City of Stoke-on-Trent', takes water.

(*Below*) The driver of rebuilt Royal Scot no. 46122, 'Royal Ulster Rifleman', waits for the right-away at Crewe watched by three spotters. Judging by the quality of the coal in the tender the fireman could be in for a rough trip.

(*Right*) Princess Royal Pacific no. 46205, 'Princess Victoria', pauses at Nuneaton with an up express in 1949.

(*Below*) Is it a 'cop'? The station authorities seem to have turned a blind eye to the crowd of spotters at the north end of Crewe station watching rebuilt Scot no. 46101, 'Royal Scots Grey', arriving with a Euston express.

NAMED TRAINS

(*Left*) Its safety valves lifting, Coronation Pacific no. 46244, 'King George VI', speeds down Shap with the 'Caledonian' bound for Euston where it is due to arrive at 3.40 pm, after a 7 hour 10 minute journey from Glasgow Central.

(*Below left*) The 'Red Rose' which left Euston for Liverpool at 12.5 pm was regularly worked by the Princess Royal class. Here no. 46200, 'The Princess Royal', leaking badly at the front end, pounds past Bourne End box. In 1961 the train took just over 4 hours to reach Liverpool, compared with a typical present day timing of 2 hours 40 minutes.

(*Below*) Coronation Pacific no. 46256, 'Sir William A. Stanier F.R.S.', is just restarting the up 'Royal Scot' from Bletchley after a special stop for water, possibly because its tender scoop was out of action or Castlethorpe troughs were under repair.

(*Above*) The down 'Mid-day Scot' passes Leighton Buzzard in charge of Princess Royal Pacific no. 46212, 'Duchess of Kent'. In 1951 this train left Euston at 1.15 pm.

(*Above*) Only two of the 191 Jubilee class were rebuilt with a no. 2A boiler and double chimney – nos 5735 and 5736. Working from Camden shed they were used on top class trains. Here one of the pair, no. 45736, 'Phoenix', is approaching Bletchley with the down 'Ulster Express'.

(*Left*) The 'Comet' ran between Euston and Manchester in a fraction under 4 hours on weekdays, and by using it the businessman could have about the same time in the Lancashire capital before returning home. Longsight Britannia no. 70043, 'Thomas Hardy', is, unusually, on the down slow line at Hemel Hempstead and Boxmoor with the northbound train.

(*Above*) The down 'Manxman' passing through Roade cutting on its way to Liverpool Lime Street behind Jubilee no. 45643, 'Rodney'. On the left is the massive steel and brickwork structure forming the route for the diverging line to Northampton.

(*Above*) The 'Mancunian' was the Lancashire businessman's equivalent to the 'Comet'. The up train is passing King's Langley behind Britannia Pacific no. 70043, 'Lord Kitchener', on the last stage of its journey to Euston where it will arrive at 1.40 pm.

THE 'ROYAL SCOT'

(*Above*) A lowly pick-up freight headed by 4F no. 44399 stands in the loop at Thrimby Grange to allow the up 'Royal Scot' to pass with Coronation Pacific no. 46247, 'City of Liverpool'.

(*Right*) Also at Thrimby Grange, the trip working to Tebay waits in the loop as the down 'Royal Scot' sweeps past on the descent from Shap behind Coronation Pacific no. 46250, 'City of Lichfield'.

(*Left*) The down 'Royal Scot' passing closed Grayrigg station behind Coronation Pacific no. 46256, 'Sir William A. Stanier F.R.S.'.

THE PRINCESS ROYALS

(*Right*) No. 46204, 'Princess Louise', making up time through Tring cutting with the 2.10 pm Liverpool–Euston express. Tring cutting with its high sides could be very hot on a summer day and I remember walking along the cess with my handkerchief knotted at the four corners, fireman's style, against the worst of the heat.

(*Below*) The freedom of the northern hills comes over strongly in this picture of no. 46209, 'Princess Beatrice', climbing Shap past Scout Green with the 10.40 am Euston–Carlisle–Perth train.

(*Left*) The driver of rebuilt Scot no. 46122, 'Royal Ulster Rifleman', opens the regulator for the start out of Crewe with a down train.

(*Right*) Another rebuilt Scot no. 46108, 'Seaforth Highlander', speeds past upper quadrant signals at Bletchley on a northbound train – the loco shed is on the right.

(*Below*) Coronation Pacific no. 46224, 'Princess Alexandra', passes a curiously angled upper quadrant signal at Watford Junction with a Glasgow train.

LNWR SIGNAL BOXES

(*Above*) Looking very rundown, streamlined Pacific no. 6243, 'City of Lancaster', passes Tring No. 1 box on a Liverpool–Euston express in 1946.

(*Above left*) Class 5 no. 45147, heading an extra formed of various types of coaches, passes Tring No. 2 signal-box.

(*Left*) Bletchley No. 3 signal-box towers over rebuilt Scot no. 46122, 'Royal Ulster Rifleman', heading a Wolverhampton–Euston express. In the shed scrap road Fowler 2–6–2T no. 40002 and a 4F 0–6–0 await disposal. No. 40002 was withdrawn in 1959 and the whole class had gone by 1962.

(*Above*) The signalman fills in his train register book in Tring No. 2 box.

A contrast in freight power at Bletchley. In 1952 Stanier 8F no. 48420 waits for admission to the yard whilst an LNWR G2a 0–8–0 heads north with mineral empties. The name of that year's Derby winner, the Aga Khan's 'Tulyar', is chalked on the side of the cab of the 8F, unknowingly anticipating the arrival of Deltic diesel no. 55.015.

CLASS 5s AT BLETCHLEY

(*Right*) A Manchester–Willesden freight passes Bletchley behind no. 44749, one of an experimental batch built in 1948 and fitted with Caprotti valve gear and roller bearings.

(*Below*) Monument Lane's no. 44766 comes under Bletchley flyover with a train for Euston. This locomotive was built in 1947 and fitted with roller bearings and a double chimney.

(*Right*) No. 45439 is approaching Bletchley with a Sunday morning excursion to Euston, whilst on the right Jubilee no. 45676, 'Codrington', is waiting to leave the sidings with a parcels train.

(*Below*) No. 44711 of Rugby shed makes a vigorous start from Bletchley with a Rugby via Northampton–Euston train in May 1955.

MORNING LIGHT

(*Left*) Bright morning sun could be relied on to give attractive pictures as these two pages show – Coronation Pacific no. 46256, 'Sir William A. Stanier F.R.S.', passing Bletchley with the down Royal Scot. The shortened cab side sheets show up especially well in this picture.

(*Left*) Rebuilt Scot no. 46135, 'The East Lancashire Regiment', passing Eden Valley junction with the 8.30 am Carlisle–Euston train. The North Eastern line to Barnard Castle bears off to the right.

(*Above*) A striking picture of Jubilee no. 45582, 'Central Provinces', overtaking a slow train to Bletchley north of Apsley.

JUBILEES ON VARIED DUTIES

(*Above left*) No. 45604, 'Ceylon', is halted at closed Clifton and Lowther station by a 'stop and examine' message from Penrith.

(*Below left*) No doubt because of the photographic attraction of the famous incline, Shap station was rarely pictured. This pre-war shot finds no. 5691, 'Orion', passing with a Glasgow–Liverpool express. Over 800 feet above sea level, the station's situation was the highest between Euston and Carlisle.

(*Right*) No. 45555, 'Quebec', looks out of place on a local freight for Kingmoor Yard leaving Penrith.

(*Above*) On a wet afternoon at Bletchley, Camden's no. 45672, 'Anson', pulls slowly out of the station with a vans train for Euston.

(*Above*) A picture full of Midland Railway atmosphere – Compound 4–4–0 no. 41032, originally built in 1906 and rebuilt in 1926, passes Great Glen station on an express for St Pancras in 1949.

COMPOUNDS

(*Right*) Until the advent of the British Railways Standard types in the early 1950s, the Compounds could still be seen on express duties. No. 41084, one of the batch built by the LMS in 1924, passes Mill Hill northbound from St Pancras.

(*Left*) A 1930s picture of no. 1051 passing West Hampstead with a slow train for St Pancras.

(*Below*) Bletchley looks its most dismal as no. 41122 leaves for Euston under a small gantry of LNWR signals in 1954.

2P 4–4–0s

(*Above*) One of the original batch of class 2 4–4–0s no. 40482 built by the Midland Railway runs into Crewe with a stopping train from Manchester. The p.w. gang seems indifferent to the train's arrival – no high visibility vests in those days!

(*Left*) Another of the original batch, no. 40551 of Bedford shed, leaves Bletchley with a train for Oxford.

(*Above*) Stafford 2P no. 40646 makes an attractive picture at Shrewsbury in between duties.

(*Below*) The earlier batch of engines had 7-foot driving wheels. Here no. 40511 attaches a van to a northbound train at Birmingham New Street.

35

DOUBLE-HEADED

(*Right*) Even in the years just after the war when fifteen-coach trains were commonplace on the LMS, double-heading by Royal Scots was rare. However, such is the case here as two very dirty members of the class, no. 6101, 'Royal Scots Grey', in rebuilt condition and no. 6148, 'The Manchester Regiment', pull out of Crewe for Euston.

(*Below*) A pair of 2P 4–4–0s, no. 538 still in LMS livery and no. 40539, work the 1 pm Leicester–Kettering train near Great Glen in July 1948.

(*Above*) On a pouring wet day at Tebay, a Fowler 2–6–4T no. 42378 assisting a class 5 makes a dash for Shap with a very long parcels train. On such days I would get soaked on one side walking up Shap, and then on the other coming down!

(*Left*) It was not until 1955 that the last Royal Scot was rebuilt with a type 2A boiler and double chimney. No. 46163, 'Civil Service Rifleman', which was treated in 1953, is leaving Bletchley with the 8.30 am Carlisle–Euston train with a rebuilt member of the same class behind.

REBUILT SCOTS

(*Above*) Rebuilt Royal Scot no. 6124, 'London Scottish', waits to leave Crewe with an express from Blackpool to Euston.

(*Left*) A 'Black Beauty' at Crewe in 1947. No. 6146, 'The Rifle Brigade', looks particularly attractive in its post-war LMS black livery on the up-side middle road with a Euston train.

(*Above right*) No. 46133, 'The Green Howards', accelerates through Bletchley with a morning down train after a signal check.

(*Below right*) No. 46106, 'Gordon Highlander', fitted with straight smoke deflectors near King's Langley with the down 'Comet' express for Manchester.

In the gloom of a November day, rebuilt Scot no. 46139, 'The Welch Regiment', pulls out of Bletchley with the 10.35 am train from Euston to Blackpool.

THE PRINCESS CORONATIONS

(*Above*) The 1.25 pm Anglo-Scottish express approaches King's Langley, in charge is no. 46238, 'City of Carlisle', in red livery.

(*Above left*) An immaculate green-liveried Coronation Pacific no. 46228, 'Duchess of Rutland', leaves Carnforth with the morning Carlisle–Euston train in July 1957.

(*Below left*) In contrast, no. 6244, 'King George VI', is in LMS black livery as it waits to leave Crewe with a running-in turn.

(*Above*) No. 46246, 'City of Manchester', waits to leave Shrewsbury for Crewe with a running in turn.

LIGHT AND SHADE

(*Above left*) A pleasing late 1940s picture of St Pancras with passengers waiting for the empty stock of their train. The shafts of sunlight through the smoke add to the cathedral-like atmosphere.

(*Below left*) Just outside the huge train shed grimy Compound no. 1042 stokes up before departure with a slow train to Bedford.

(*Right*) Down the road at Euston sunlight and shadow set off the distinctive shape of an old Johnson 0–6–0, no. 3561, on empty carriage duties.

(*Above*) Mid-afternoon sees Fowler 2–6–4T no. 2341 and 2–6–2T no. 28 (fitted with condensing apparatus for working to Moorgate) at St Pancras during a pause between duties.

ROYAL MAIL

(*Above*) An unrebuilt Patriot waits to leave Watford Junction after mail bags have been unloaded. For a short period in 1949 these CLC coaches were used on outer London suburban services.

(*Below*) A class 5 4–6–0 and mail bags seen through the window of an LNWR electric train at Euston.

These three pictures are a reminder of the collection of mail by lineside apparatus, now a thing of the past. (*Above*) Jubilee no. 45553, 'Canada', near Lancaster with the 4.05 pm Glasgow–Manchester express. (*Right*) The postman waits for the 'West Coast Postal' near Bletchley (note the strings to keep the bag in place). (*Below*) A Jubilee no. 45634, 'Trinidad', passes pick-up apparatus on the West Coast Main Line.

WATER TROUGHS AND COLUMNS

(*Left*) Rebuilt Patriot no. 5528 pulls out of Crewe past a water column.

(*Below*) Amid the lonely fells unrebuilt Scot no. 46130, 'The West Yorkshire Regiment', takes water from Dillicar troughs with a down express. To walk along the slippery old sleepers by the troughs with a camera was a hazardous business.

(*Above*) The 7 pm slow Carlisle to Warrington train was a very easy job for a Coronation Pacific. In this striking picture no. 46233, 'Duchess of Sutherland', pulls out of Tebay (where it was due at 8.06 pm) past the water column at the south end of the station.

(*Left*) Dillicar troughs looking towards Low Gill. The 'X' sign on the left was illuminated at night to tell enginemen when to lower their tender water scoop.

TAKING WATER

(*Above*) In the early 1960s the Coronation Pacifics were often to be seen on secondary duties as diesels took over the top link work. Here no. 46243, 'City of Lancaster', takes water in the down loop at Tebay whilst on a fitted freight.

(*Right*) Rebuilt Patriot no. 45532, 'Illustrious', picks up water from Castlethorpe troughs north of Bletchley with an up train from Liverpool.

(*Top*) Jubilee no. 45688, 'Polyphemus', fills up its tender from the baronial style water tower on the up line at Penrith station.

(*Right*) This picture of 2–6–4T no. 42573 shows the 6-inch super elevation of the track at this point, while (*inset*) at the top of a column in the station a blackbird sits on her nest quite oblivious to the noise of the passing trains. I took this picture at the request of the manageress of the station buffet, and had to climb a wheeled platform ladder to do so.

PERMANENT WAY MEN

(*Left*) Permanent way workers take a break to watch unrebuilt Patriot no. 45511, 'Isle of Man', making a vigorous start from Penrith with an up freight.

(*Below*) The smoke and grime of the post-war railway is clearly seen in this 1947 picture of no. 6235, 'City of Birmingham', waiting to leave Crewe for Euston with a train from Blackpool.

(*Above*) Class 5 no. 45254 leaves Penrith with a vans train in 1951.

(*Below*) Jubilee no. 45702, 'Colossus', pulls out of Penrith for the south with a smart train of red and cream stock, as permanent way men attend to the down main line.

(*Above*) Preston unrebuilt Patriot no. 45508 hurries through Tebay station en route to a freight train runaway accident at Calthwaite, north of Penrith.

TROUBLE ON THE LINE

(*Right and above right*) The result of the smash at Calthwaite.

(*Below*) 8F no. 48207 rumbles out of
the yard at Bletchley on the way to a
weekend lifting job. The engineer
in charge had time to chase spotters
away from the lineside and to ask
to see my permit!

REPAIRS AND DIVERSIONS

(Above) Coronation Pacific no. 46223, 'Princess Alice', is about to drop the pilotman off by Tebay No. 1 box and regain the down line.

(Left) A p.w. gang at work in the Appleby district on the Settle–Carlisle line.

(Right) Coronation Pacific no. 46239, 'City of Chester', passes through Crewe station with the up 'Royal Scot'.

(*Left*) The track works on the down line at Dillicar troughs which caused the diversion shown opposite, above. This photograph gives a good impression of the miserable conditions p.w. men had to put up with at times.

(*Right*) A pre-Grouping relic at Eden Valley Junction, marking the boundary between the end of the North Eastern territory on the branch from Barnard Castle and the LNWR line to Penrith. The difference in the quality of the sleepers and ballast is notable!

(Below left, and above) A p.w. gang at work installing a new waybeam on a bridge near Appleby.

(Above left) A Crab 2–6–0 no. 42819 brings a freight train past a p.w. bothy near Appleby with a Settle–Carlisle line freight.

(Right) P.w. men in a van wait to travel to Griseburn on a Sunday morning job. Their boots are unlikely to look so highly polished at the end of the day!

ON SHED

(*Right*) At the side of Bedford shed an old Midland Railway Pullman serves as a mess room.

(*Left*) A travel stained Jubilee no. 45652, 'Hawke', waits at Bedford shed to work a stopping train to St Pancras – an avian namesake hovers in the sky above!

(*Right*) A driver oils the motion of a class 5 4–6–0 before setting off from Bletchley to work a parcels train to Marylebone via Verney Junction.

(*Below*) A tough old LNWR Cauliflower 0–6–0 no. 28555 (later no. 58413) from Workington shed, is turned at Penrith in readiness to work a train over the beautiful line to Cockermouth. These engines were long associated with this line, the last of the class going for scrap in 1955.

TEBAY

(*Above*) Fowler 2–6–4T no. 42424 standing in the shed yard at Tebay with the railway staff cottages forming a background against Tebay Fell. At the time this picture was taken no. 42424 was regarded as the best banking engine at the shed.

(*Left*) The Tebay railway staff in 1950. Fifth from left is the son of George Grayland, a signalman at Shap summit box, and fourth from the right, James O'Neill, a signalman in Tebay No. 2 box. The stationmaster is standing under the 'Y' in 'Tebay'.

(*Above*) A year or two after the picture of no. 42424 was taken, Stanier 2–6–4T no. 42110 had arrived at Tebay to help out with banking duties. She is taking water outside the shed before starting work.

(*Below*) One of Preston's unrebuilt Patriots no. 45502, 'Royal Naval Division', waits in the yard at Tebay for the arrival of a Durham miner's special which it will work to Morecambe.

(*Above*) Early morning rain is brewing in the fells as class 5 no. 45025 pulls slowly through the station with a freight. Fowler 2–6–4T no. 42424 waits to give banking assistance. No. 45025 is now preserved on the Strathspey Railway in Scotland.

(*Right*) LNWR G2a 0–8–0s at work on Shap. (*Above right*) No. 49154 on the last mile or so of the 1 in 75. (*Below right*) One of the class stokes up ready for the climb from Loups Fell just north of Tebay station.

SPECIAL TRAFFIC

(*Left*) Horse box traffic is now only a memory, but in this picture taken at 'Scotty Brig' on Shap where the road from Orton to Greenholme crosses the line, rebuilt Scot no. 46162, 'Queen's Westminster Rifleman', has six in tow.

(*Left*) Towards the end of her career, Coronation Pacific no. 46234, 'Duchess of Abercorn', hurries a milk tank train through Tebay. Class 5 no. 45307 is standing in the down loop taking water.

(*Right*) An early morning picture of rebuilt Scot no. 46128, 'The Lovat Scouts', getting to grips with the 1 in 75 of Shap near Loups Fell with a northbound milk tanks train. The engine has taken its fill on Dillicar troughs as water can be seen pouring off the tender onto the first milk tanker.

(*Below*) With a long train of Ford cars from Halewood, Speke Junction, class 5 no. 45386 pulls slowly out of the sidings at Tebay. The fireman has the sanders on, and by the expression his face sems to be looking forward to the assault on Shap.

CLASS 5s ON FREIGHT

(*Right*) No. 45296 reaches the top of Shap with a down freight.

(*Below*) On a bright morning after a night of rain, a class 5 approaches Tebay with a freight from the south.

(*Above*) On the north side of Shap, no. 45276 approaches the station with an up freight.

(*Below*) Mist covers Mallerstang Common as no. 44815 climbs towards Ais Gill with an up freight. Wild Boar Fell looms over the line in the background.

SETTLE AND CARLISLE

(*Above*) An evocative picture of Scottish based Jubilee no. 45729, 'Furious', as it waits to leave Garsdale with a slow Bradford–Carlisle train. The fireman has built up a good fire for the last part of the 'Long Drag' to Ais Gill summit, some 3 miles to the north.

(*Above right*) Britannia no. 70053, 'Moray Firth', approaching Dent Head signal-box with a northbound train.

(*Below right*) The 'Thames–Clyde' express approaching Bedford double-headed, as was sometimes the case, by a Compound and rebuilt Scot. The train was due off Carlisle just after midday, and arrived at St Pancras some 7 hours later.

(*Above*) Late on a beautiful afternoon, 9F no. 92151 approaches Garsdale station with a southbound freight. The Hawes branch comes in from the right.

(*Left*) A mineral train from Long Meg sidings to Widnes approaches Blea Moor tunnel mouth behind 8F no. 48321. The engine is climbing at 1 in 440 at this point, but when it emerges from the other side 1 mile 869 yards later it will be descending the ruling 1 in 100 gradient towards Settle. Dent Head viaduct can be seen above the engine's tender, and Dent Head box beyond.

(*Above*) 4F no. 44181 climbs towards Rise Hill tunnel with a northbound freight. This picture gives a good impression of the rugged open country which gives the Settle–Carlisle line its universal appeal.

(*Right*) The 4.25 pm Hawes–Hellifield train leaves Garsdale behind 2–6–4T no. 42648. I was told by a member of the station staff at Garsdale that the train had gained its traditional name, 'Bonnyface', from the workers in the fields along the line, since the time of its passing meant that the day's toil was almost over.

Three pictures taken on the Settle–Carlisle line. (*Left*) The stationmaster and staff at the windswept Garsdale station. (*Inset below*) Blea Moor tunnel looking north towards the maintenance staff huts on the right. (*Bottom*) Ribblehead station with Whernside, 2,414 feet, in the background. Note the wind speed and direction indicator adjacent to the up platform – the station was a meteorological reporting point from which the stationmaster sent out information, for which he was given special training.

(*Above*) Carrying his paraffin can, the lamp boy at Denthead signal-box has almost completed his walk from Dent station. The signalman reads his paper in the box no doubt enjoying the fresh moorland air.

(*Below*) Some 9 miles to the north at the summit of the Settle–Carlisle line at Ais Gill, 1,167 feet above sea level, the local goods to Hellifield stops so that the guard can hand water supplies to the signalman.

MIDLAND AND LNWR SIGNAL BOXES

(*Left*) Midland Railway features abound in this picture of Standard class 5 no. 73003 passing Oakley station with a St Pancras train.

(*Below*) A Wellingborough 9F no. 92059 storms past Ampthill signal-box with a freight for Brent sidings.

(*Above right*) Compared with Midland Railway signal-boxes, the LNWR variety were severe in outline. At Garstang and Catterall 9½ miles north of Preston, Ivatt 2–6–0 no. 46487 is in charge of an Inspecting Officer's saloon.

(*Below right*) Class 5 no. 45258 passes Lancaster No. 1 box and an Ivatt 2–6–0 – the line diverging to the right led to the original Lancaster and Preston Railway Penny Street station.

SHAP SIGNAL-MEN

(*Above*) Coronation Pacific no. 46251, 'City of Nottingham', passes Scout Green box with the morning Perth–Euston train in 1949. The model aircraft on the post in the left foreground was made by the signalman in the picture, but it disappeared in the 1950s.

(*Right*) The 5 pm Oxenholme–Carlisle local train hurries past Scout Green box behind 2–6–4T no. 42573 due to a late start. The tall LNWR up signal was always a favourite subject for photographers, though its sheer height could cause problems in the viewfinder.

Two well-known signalmen. (*Left*) James O'Neill at Tebay no. 2 box. (*Below*) George Grayland at Shap summit box. Both were good friends to those holding lineside passes for photography. Sadly, James died suddenly. George, who retired in 1955, began work in the box as a relief signalman in 1913. He was a man of many parts, building himself a wind-driven generator. He also trained a fox to accept a dog's lead and to accompany him on walks.

SHAP SUMMIT AND LAMBRIGG

(*Right*) Another picture of the interior of Shap summit box.

(*Below*) The down Royal Scot passes the summit on a wet day behind Coronation Pacific no. 46247, 'City of Liverpool'.

ROYAL SCOT
46247

(*Above*) Fowler 2–6–4T no. 42314 passing Lambrigg Crossing box with the midday Saturdays Only Oxenholme–Carlisle stopping train.

(*Left*) In later years the window by the signal-box door was protected from lumps of coal falling off locomotive tenders by a strong mesh screen.

LUNE GORGE

(*Left*) The 5 pm Oxenholme–Carlisle slow train near Dillicar behind a 2–6–4T.

(*Right*) The Clapham line diverges to the right as West Auckland's Standard class 4 no. 76024 passes Low Gill with a train from the North East Region to the Fylde coast.

(*Left*) Before the M6 changed the landscape, Joseph Locke's way up Shap taken from Grayrigg Forest looking across to Orton Scar and Cross Fell, 2,930 feet. A plume of steam marks the passage of a train up Shap in the distance.

(*Right*) An old Midland Railway warrior, 3F no. 3137, on a Tebay–Clapham goods at Low Gill on a wet day in 1946. This train was nicknamed 'The Nibble'un' – a little at a time!

THE SHAP BANKERS

(*Left, and below left*) Two views of an Ivatt 2–6–0 buffering up to a freight at Tebay. These two pictures give some idea of how busy the line was shortly after the war. Another freight waits its turn in the station.

Pictures taken from the cab of a Shap banker. (*Right*) The driver's view from a Fowler 2–6–4T. (*Below*) The crew of a Stanier 2–6–4T.

(*Left*) A Fowler 2–6–4T prepares to buffer up to a freight at Tebay, the gradient at this point being 1 in 146. The attractive LNWR signals in the picture on the right have been replaced by LMS upper quadrants.
(*Below left*) The engine starts banking work in earnest.

(*Right*) An evening scene at Tebay as a freight sets off up the bank, and local residents use the track to reach the station.

(*Right*) A Stanier 2–6–4T banks a freight past Loups Fell staff cottages.

(*Above*) A guard's view from the rear of a freight train.

FREIGHT ON SHAP

(*Above*) Class 5 no. 45422 slowly starts the climb up Shap with the banker pushing from behind. The North Eastern sidings can be seen to the left of the engine.

(*Left*) A Stanier 2–6–4T working light engine coasts down Shap near Scout Green as a northbound freight plods uphill.

(*Above right*) The panorama from the south end of the cutting leading to Shap summit with Langdale Fell in the distance.

(*Below right*) Class 5 no. 45235 climbs powerfully past Scout Green box with a northbound freight. By this time the tall LNWR up signal had been replaced with a colour light.

(*Left*) On a warm summer afternoon Bushbury class 5 no. 45405 sends up a fine exhaust climbing Shap with a freight.

(*Right*) A Fowler 2–6–4T assists a train of empty mineral wagons past Scout Green. Note the careful edging between the cess and the ballast which was a requirement in Coronation year.

(*Below*) The early morning sun looks likely to give way to rain in this view of a northbound freight taken from the Junction Hotel at Tebay. In the foreground are some of the staff cottages for the local railway workers.

THE PRINCESS CORONATIONS
AT WORK

(*Above*) Coronation Pacific no. 46236, 'City of Bradford', collects through coaches from Windermere to Euston at Oxenholme for attachment to its train on the right of the picture.

(*Right*) In a haze of brake dust, the 8.30 am Carlisle–Euston train arrives at Tebay behind no. 6240, 'City of Coventry'.

(*Above*) No. 6234, 'Duchess of Abercorn', has at least fifteen coaches on as she tackles the rise through Wigan with an Anglo-Scottish express.

(*Right*) On a tender with a coal capacity of 10 tons, the fireman needed some help in bringing the coal forward – the steam operated coal pusher is in use as no. 46233, 'Duchess of Sutherland', passes Shap summit with a southbound express. The coaches on the right were for the granite quarry workers' train to Penrith which was usually powered by a Tebay engine.

THE VARIED SCENE AT TEBAY

(*Above*) In pouring rain Jubilee no. 45719, 'Glorious', speeds through a deserted looking Tebay with a down train.

(*Left*) In September 1950 4F no. 44292 turns into the NER yard at Tebay with a train of empty mineral wagons.

(*Above right*) The fine condition of the permanent way can be appreciated in this picture of Britannia no. 70043, 'Lord Kitchener', starting the climb out of Tebay.

(*Right*) Another Britannia no. 70017, 'Arrow', slows for a stop at Tebay with a southbound parcels train. The line crosses the River Lune at this point.

95

THE STANDARD TYPES ARRIVE

(*Left*) The British Railways Standard types came too late on the London Midland scene to have much impact, but nevertheless they put in some useful work. In this picture Polmadie Clan no. 72003, 'Clan Fraser', climbs past Scout Green with a Birmingham–Glasgow express.

(*Below*) Britannia no. 70052, 'Firth of Tay', pulls slowly out of Lancaster with a Glasgow train.

(*Above*) Standard class 4 2–6–4T no. 80043 is in charge of a slow train to Bletchley near Leighton Buzzard.

(*Below*) Then only a few weeks old, Bedford Standard class 4 4–6–0 no. 75041 departs from Bletchley with an Oxford train. D16/3 no. 62585 has brought in a train from Cambridge.

CLASS 5s ON PASSENGER WORKINGS

(*Above*) Happily class 5 no. 45379, one of the Armstrong Whitworth engines, has been preserved and is at the Bitton Railway Centre, Bristol. Here she is leaving Peterborough East.

(*Above left*) In 1946 before the age of the pleasure cruiser, working barges were a commonplace sight on the Grand Union Canal. A class 5 heads a down semi-fast train near Berkhamsted.

(*Left*) The small LNWR signal makes a striking contrast to the then modern lines of class 5 no. 5400 at Willesden Junction just before the last war. This engine was built by Armstrong Whitworth in 1937.

JUBILEES ON EXPRESS DUTY

(*Right*) Preserved Jubilee no. 45690, 'Leander', passing under the Bletchley flyover. I am at a loss to explain what appears to be a 52E shedplate, Percy Main. Maybe this code was re-allocated to a more likely shed at some time.

(*Above right*) Just after nationalisation in 1948 three Jubilees were painted experimentally in a light green livery with Sans Serif smokebox door numbers. One of the trio (the others were nos 45604 and 45694) no. 45565, 'Victoria', is on an up express near Mill Hill on the Midland main line.

(*Below right*) In the event Brunswick green was adopted for express engines, and no. 45685, 'Barfleur', is seen in this livery waiting to leave Sheffield Midland with the down 'Thames–Clyde' express.

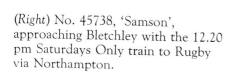

(*Above*) A St Pancras–Derby express passing 3F no. 43829 at St Albans behind no. 45554, 'Ontario'.

(*Right*) No. 45738, 'Samson', approaching Bletchley with the 12.20 pm Saturdays Only train to Rugby via Northampton.

FIRST IN THE CLASS

(*Above*) Rebuilt Scot no. 46100, 'Royal Scot', on the 1.35 pm Euston–Blackpool train at Hunton Bridge. The locomotive was in fact the original no. 6152, and the plate below the name records no. 6100's visit to Canada and the USA in 1933.

(*Above left*) Although ostensibly the first of the class, no. 5552, 'Silver Jubilee', was in fact the original no. 5642, the change taking place in 1935. Still with its chromium plated numbers and tender lettering, no. 5552 is on a Euston–Birmingham train near King's Langley.

(*Below left*) The only 8P Standard locomotive no. 71000, 'Duke of Gloucester', with a northbound train passing Scout Green box.

SIGNALS

(*Right*) Rebuilt Scot no. 46146, 'The Rifle Brigade', speeds through Bletchley with the 10.50 am Birkenhead–Chester–Euston train.

(*Below*) Signals at Tebay on the approach from Kirkby Stephen. On the left is an LMS upper quadrant controlling the entrance to the LM yard, the centre signal is LNWR, and that on the right a fine example of an NER distant.

(*Above*) The famous signal gantry at Preston looking north in 1952. The signals on the left control the traffic to Fleetwood and Blackpool, whilst the others are for the main line to the north and the Longridge branch on the far right.

(*Right*) The smoke clinging about the top of the smokebox emphasises the massive proportions of unrebuilt Scot no. 6151, 'The Royal Horse Guardsman', as it passes upper quadrant signals at Northchurch box in 1947.

(*Above*) Jubilee no. 45698, 'Mars', coasts down from Shap summit past Thrimby Grange box and its LNWR signals with a northbound train. The trip working from Penrith waits for the up road by the box. During times like this the crew would sometimes pick mushrooms in the adjacent field.

(*Below*) Unrebuilt Patriot no. 45524, 'Blackpool', accelerates hard out of Penrith with an up express.

(Above) LNWR G2a 0–8–0 no. 49061 prepares to enter Bletchley yard with a mineral train from the north.

(Left) A strong easterly wind catches the smoke of unrebuilt Scot no. 46156, 'The South Wales Borderer', as it roars past Sears Crossing signalbox with an up train.

UNREBUILT PATRIOTS

(*Above*) A blustery day at Leighton Buzzard as no. 45511, 'Isle of Man', heads into the wind with a freight train for Willesden.

(*Above right*) Another view of Sears Crossing box with no. 45507, 'Royal Tank Corps', passing with an up express.

(*Right*) No. 45537, 'Private E. Sykes, V.C.', in early nationalisation days. The locomotive is waiting at Oxenholme for the connection from Euston to arrive.

VETERANS AT WORK

(*Above*) Some of the LNWR
Claughton class were rebuilt with
large boilers in 1928, and one of these,
no. 6004, outlasted her sister engines
by eight years. Here she is on Dillicar
troughs with a down fitted freight.
Judging by the clouds of black smoke
the engine may be in trouble for
steam and will no doubt stop at
Tebay for assistance.

(*Right*) One of the former LNWR
0–6–0STs allocated to Wolverton for
duty in the carriage works, in the
sidings at Bletchley shed awaiting
attention.

(*Above*) A Webb 2–4–2T no. 46601 berths eight wagons of loco coal for Leighton Buzzard shed in a siding beside the line at Linslade tunnel.

(*Below*) G2a 0–8–0 no. 9095 shunts in Warrington Bank Quay goods yard, now the site of a car park for Inter City travellers.

THE LMS MOGULS

(*Above*) A southbound fitted freight for Brent sidings north of St Albans behind Crab 2–6–0 no. 42890 which was built in 1930 at Crewe.

(*Right*) The Stanier 2–6–0 6P5F class was small in number, and the locomotives never seemed to attract much attention, but one is preserved on the Severn Valley Railway. These two pictures show them at work on the West Coast Main Line. (*Above right*) No. 2955 on a down fitted freight at Bourne End, the scene of the serious accident in 1945. (*Below right*) No. 42946 on the northbound climb to Shap near Harrison's sidings.

EIGHT-COUPLED FREIGHT

(*Left*) A Stanier 8F passes Boxmoor with a long rake of empty mineral wagons. To the left an Ivatt 2–6–0 no. 46431 shunts in the sidings.

(*Below*) A similar duty for no. 48215 passing Harpenden Junction. The line on the left was to Hemel Hempstead Midland station.

(*Above*) No. 48282, one of the 8F ex-War Department 2–8–0s built by the North British Locomotive Company in 1942 for war service heads south near Bletchley with more empty mineral wagons.

(*Right*) LNWR G2a no. 49202, an earlier generation of freight engine, pulls slowly away from Penrith with a freight for the south. The 3A Bescot shedplate poses the question as to whether the engine had really worked up from its Midlands home.

HEAVY FREIGHT

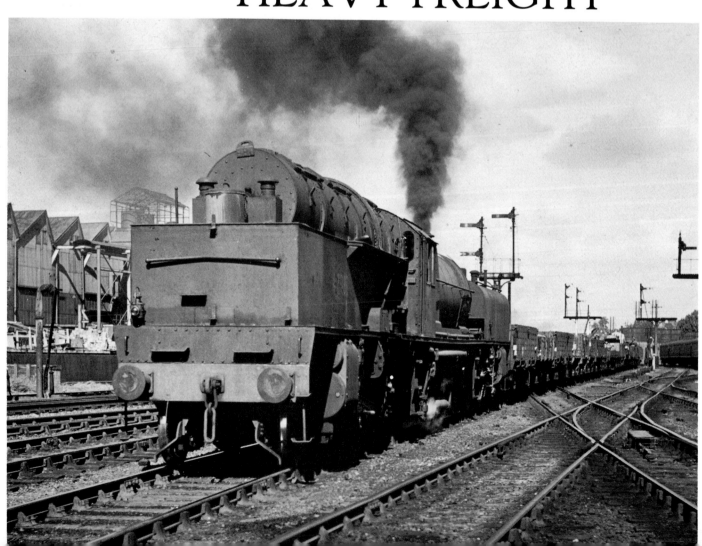

The Beyer-Garratt 2–6–0–0–6–2s were primarily built to work the slow, heavy freights on the southern section of the Midland main line, and these three pictures show them at work on their home territory. (*Left*) No. 7996 passing St Albans. (*Below left*) No. 47986 approaching St Albans showing the 9-ton rotating coal bunker. (*Right*) No. 47994 near Bedford with an up freight, whilst a Jubilee comes up on the fast line.

(*Above*) All the Garratts had gone by 1958, no. 47994 being the last. Their duties were gradually taken over by the Standard 9F 2–10–0s, although the Crosti version was inefficient and dirty. No. 92027 from Wellingborough shed passes Bedford Midland Road with an up freight – a four-wheel rail bus is on the right.

THE DIESELS ARRIVE

(*Left*) Foretelling the end of steam on local workings, a railcar stands in the shed sidings at Bletchley, while rebuilt Patriot no. 45530, 'Sir Frank Ree', passes south with an express.

(*Below*) LMS diesel no. 10001 has been relegated to freight working at Bletchley. The G2a on the right was working a train of new tube stock for delivery to London Transport.

(Above) In their heyday the pair of LMS Derby built diesels nos 10000 and 10001 worked the Royal Scot train with some success. Here they are leaving Carlisle with the up train, but what a lifeless picture!

(Right) To concentrate main line diesel power on the London Midland region, the three Southern units built at Ashford and Brighton were transferred in 1955 for use on the West Coast Main Line. The last of the trio, no. 10203, is approaching Bletchley with an up test train.

The beginning and the end. (*Above*) The up Royal Scot leaving Carlisle on the start of its journey to Euston. (*Right*) The last coach of a Euston–Manchester train disappears into Linslade tunnel.